7

16 17 18 19 20

26 27 28 29 30

36 37 38 39 40

46 47 48 49 50

56 57 58 59 60

66 67 68 69 70

76 77 78 79 80

86 87 88 89 90

96 97 98 99 100

Barbie™
Numbers
Book

1 one

2 two

3 three

LONDON, NEW YORK, MUNICH,
MELBOURNE, AND DELHI

Designer Thelma-Jane Robb
Editor Amy Junor
Senior Editor Catherine Saunders
Publishing Manager Simon Beecroft
Brand Manager Lisa Lanzarini
Category Publisher Alex Allan
Production Rochelle Talary
DTP Designer Hanna Ländin

First American Edition, 2006
06 07 08 09 10 10 9 8 7 6 5 4 3 2 1

Published in the United States by
DK Publishing, Inc.
375 Hudson Street
New York, New York 10014

Library of Congress Cataloging-in-Publication Data
Barbie numbers book.-- 1st American ed.
p. cm.
ISBN-13: 978-0-75661-857-5 (hardcover)
ISBN-10: 0-7566-1857-6
1. Counting--Juvenile literature. 2. Arithmetic--Juvenile literature.
QA113.B363 2006
513--dc22
2005036014

Reproduced by Media Development and Printing, Ltd.
Printed and bound in China by Toppan Printing Co., Ltd.

Acknowledgments
Barbie® doll photography by the Mattel Photo Studio

All other non-Barbie® images © Dorling Kindersley www.dkimages.com

Additional photography by Jon Bouchier, Paul Bricknell, Jane Burton, Gordon Clayton, Andy Crawford, Geoff Dann, Philip Dowell, Mike Dunning, Steve Gorton, Steve Gorton and Karl, Frank Greenaway, Marc Henrie, Dave King, Bill Ling, Stephen Oliver, Susanna Price, Tim Ridley, Jules Selmes, Steve Shott, James Stevenson, Harry Taylor, Matthew Ward, Barry Watts, Andrew Whittuck, and Jerry Young.

The publisher would also like to thank the staff at Mattel, Inc., especially Vicki Jaeger, Monica Okazaki, and Judy Tsuno.

Discover more at
www.dk.com

Barbie™
Numbers
Book

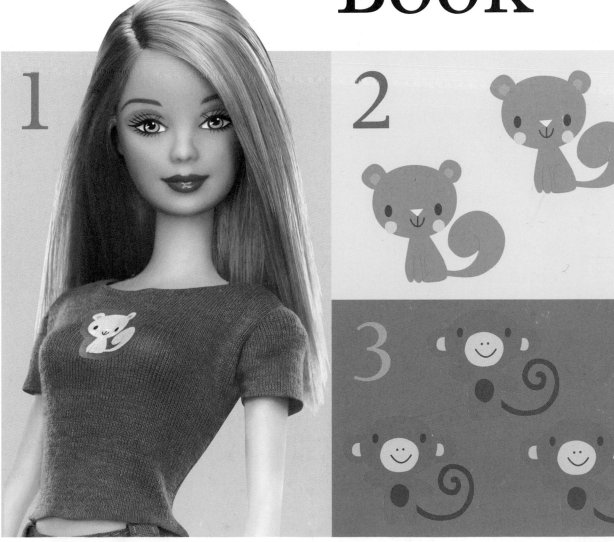

How to use this book

Barbie™ Numbers Book is the perfect way to learn about numbers and basic math. It features themes and images that children love and can relate to, such as birthday parties, baby animals, and dressing up. First of all, Barbie leads your child through basic counting, starting from one to ten and going all the way up to one hundred! Next Barbie introduces simple math problems, showing how to add, subtract, divide, and multiply. Read this book aloud and watch your child's understanding of numbers grow. And most of all, have fun!

Contents

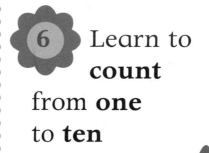

6 Learn to **count** from **one** to **ten**

8 Learn to **count** at **bedtime**

10 Mix it up!

12 **How many** baby animals?

14 **Which number** is missing?

16 Now learn to **count** from **eleven** to **twenty**!

18 Learn to **count** at a **birthday party**

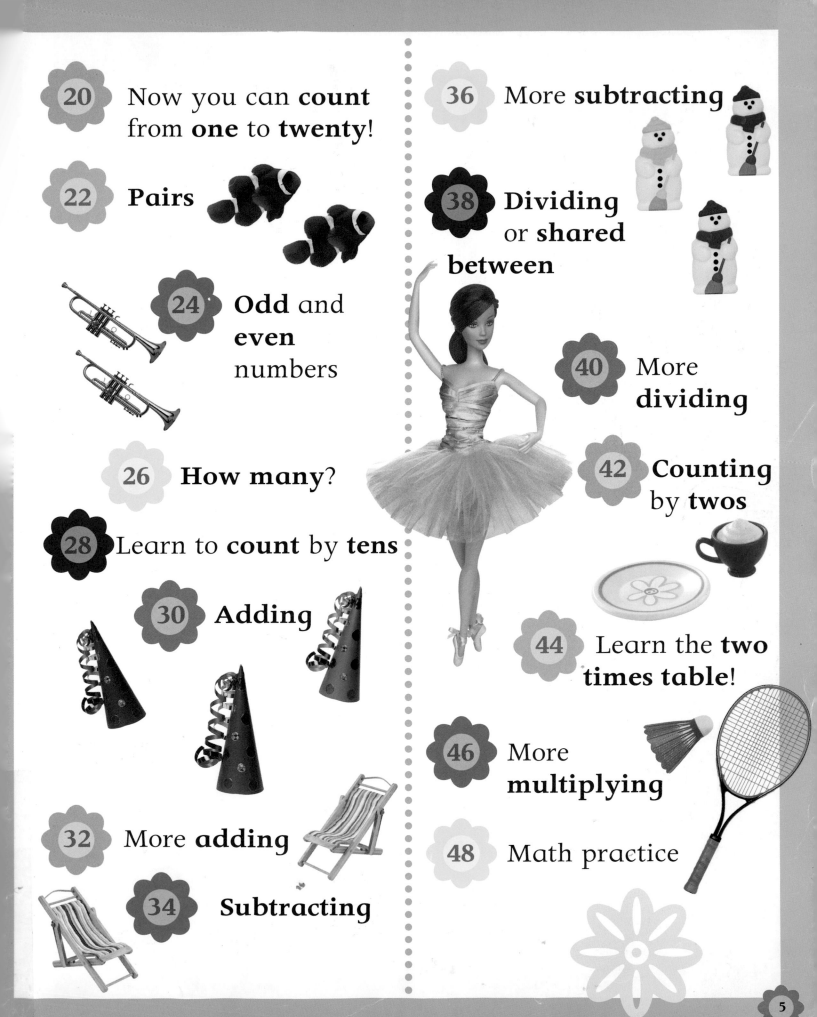

20 Now you can **count** from **one** to **twenty**!

22 Pairs

24 **Odd** and **even** numbers

26 **How many**?

28 Learn to **count** by **tens**

30 Adding

32 More **adding**

34 Subtracting

36 More **subtracting**

38 Dividing or **shared** between

40 More **dividing**

42 Counting by **twos**

44 Learn the **two** times table!

46 More **multiplying**

48 Math practice

Learn to **count** from **one** to **ten**

1 one

4 four

7 seven

9 nine

6

2 two

3 three

5 five

6 six

8 eight

Say each number out loud as you count.

10 ten

Keep practicing until you feel confident.

Learn to **count** at **bedtime**

1

closet

4

blankets

7
toothbrushes

9

lamps

2

beds

3

nightgowns

5

robes

6

clocks

8

pillows

Count these bedtime objects.

How many robes are there?

How many clocks are there?

How many lamps are there?

10

teddy bears

9

Mix it up!

6

jacket

necklaces

sweaters

hats

T-shirts

bags

2 3 4 5

7 8 9 10

coats

skirts

Match them up!

The numbers from one to ten are in the correct order, but the groups of clothes are all mixed up.

dresses

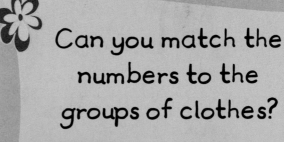

shorts

Can you match the numbers to the groups of clothes?

How many
baby animals?

8

foal

hamsters

2

piglets

1

9

4

puppies

goats

7

chicks

5

3

rabbits

10

kittens

lambs

6

Mix and match

Count the baby animals and find the number that matches.

How many kittens are there?

How many lambs are there?

calves

13

Which number is missing?

1

1

2 tiaras

3

4 tiaras

2 dresses

?

4 dresses

5

4

5 jewels

6

7 jewels

2

castles

3

4

castles

?

5

6 tiaras

?

8

tiaras

6

dresses

?

?

Find the number!

Each sequence has
a missing number.

What are the
missing numbers?
Top tip Say each sequence
out loud!

To make it harder, the
last two sequences don't
start at number one!

9

jewels

Now learn to **count** from **eleven** to **twenty**!

11 eleven

14 fourteen

17 seventeen

19 nineteen

12 twelve

13 thirteen

15 fifteen

16 sixteen

18 eighteen

20 twenty

Which number comes after eleven?

Which number comes before twenty?

17

Learn to **count** at a **birthday party**

11

birthday cakes

14

sandwiches

17

ice cream sundaes

19

lollipops

12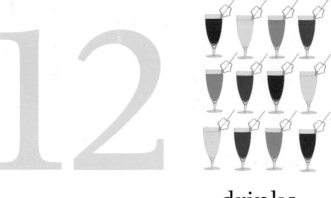

drinks

13

ice cream cones

15

pieces of candy

16

cupcakes

18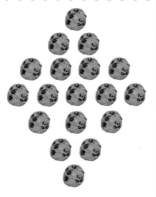

cookies

20

gumdrops

How many cupcakes are there?

How many cookies are there?

Now you can **count** from **one** to **twenty!**

1
one

2
two

6
six

7
seven

8
eight

9
nine

11
eleven

12
twelve

13
thirteen

14
fourteen

16
sixteen

17
seventeen

18
eighteen

19
nineteen

3

three

4

four

5

five

10

ten

15

fifteen

20

twenty

Now it's your turn!

It's time to put together all the things you have learned so far.

Count the numbers from one to twenty.

Which number comes after ten?

Which number comes before fifteen?

Which number comes after eight?

Pairs

2 shells

8 flippers

10 starfish

= equals

14 fish

If there are fourteen fish, how many pairs of fish are there?

=

equals

1 pair of shells

=

equals

4 pairs of flippers

5 pairs of starfish

=

equals

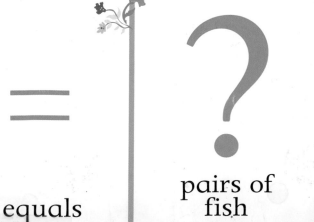

pairs of
fish

Pairs

Pairs are groups
of two objects that
look the same.

To find out how many
pairs there are, put
the objects that look
the same into
groups of two.

23

Odd and even numbers

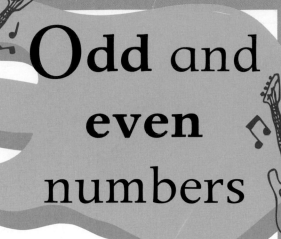

1

6 drums

7

8 trumpets

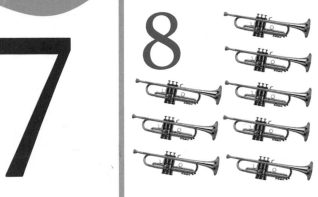

11

12 tambourines

13

16 maracas

17

18 bells

2

pianos

3

4

guitars

5

9

10

violins

Even numbers
An even number of objects can be paired up. Each even number on this page is blue and has a group of pictures beside it.

14

musical notes

15

Odd numbers
When an odd number of objects are paired up, there is always one left over. All the odd numbers on this page are pink.

19

20

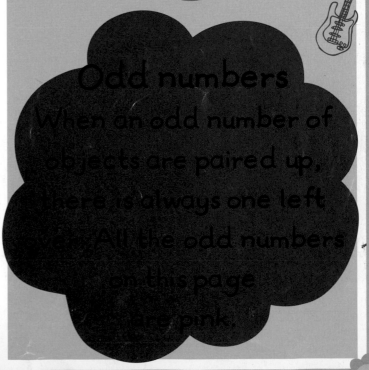

recorders

How many?

boas

dress-up box

jewelry boxes

rings

fairy wings

hats

lipsticks

masks

bags

nail polish

wands

pairs of shoes

Dress Up!
Barbie loves to dress up.

Count how many there are of each item.

Can any groups of items be paired up?

How many groups contain an odd number of items?

Learn to count by tens!

10
ten

40
forty

70
seventy

90
ninety

20

twenty

30

thirty

50

fifty

60

sixty

80

eighty

100

one hundred

Now that you can count up to twenty, look how easy it is to count by tens to one hundred!

Top tip Each of these numbers begins with one of the numbers from one to ten that you already know!

29

Adding

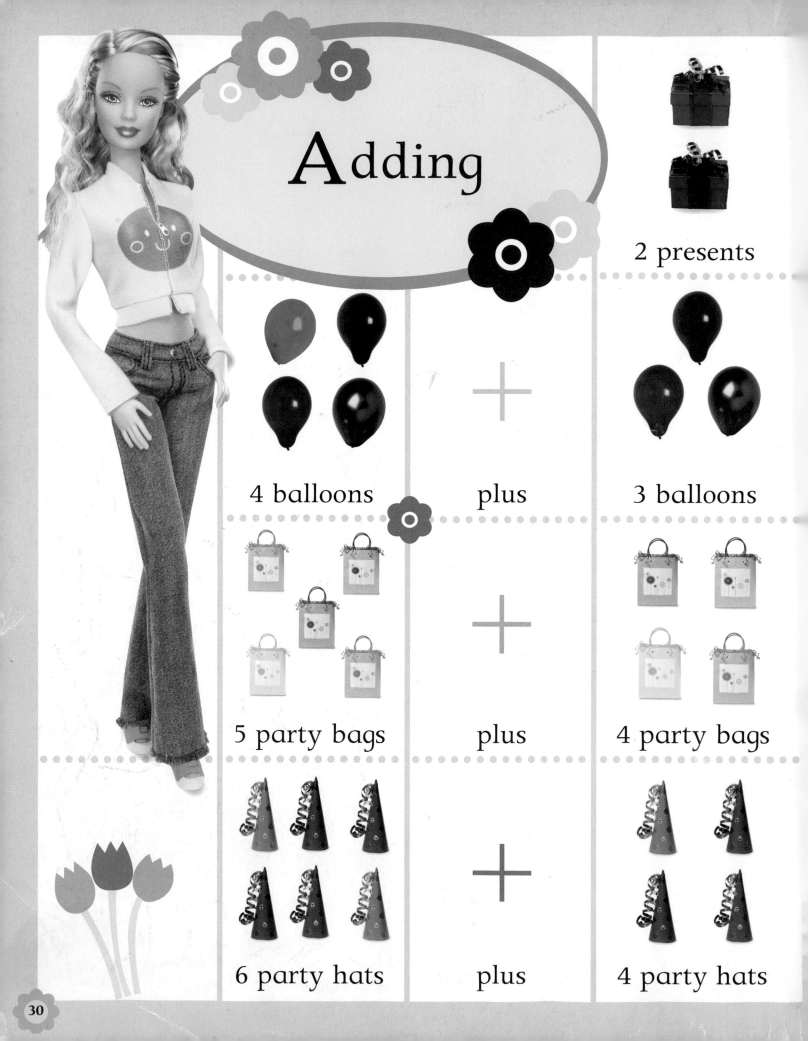

2 presents

4 balloons   plus   3 balloons

5 party bags   plus   4 party bags

6 party hats   plus   4 party hats

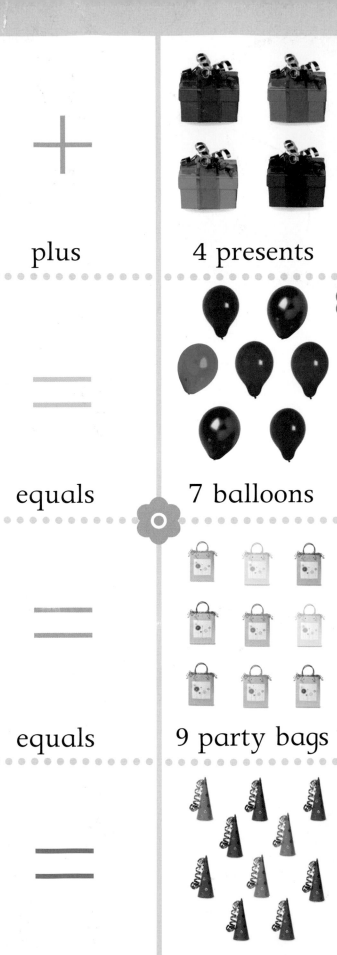

$+$

plus

4 presents

$=$

equals

6 presents

$=$

equals

7 balloons

$=$

equals

9 party bags

$=$

equals

10 party hats

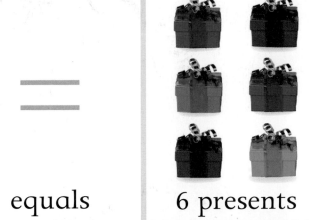

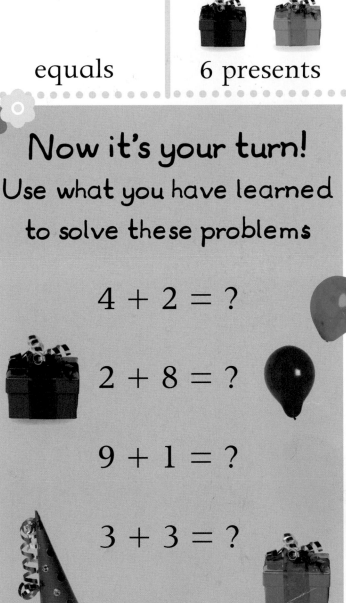

Now it's your turn!
Use what you have learned to solve these problems

$4 + 2 = ?$

$2 + 8 = ?$

$9 + 1 = ?$

$3 + 3 = ?$

$4 + 5 = ?$

$6 + 3 = ?$

$1 + 7 = ?$

More adding

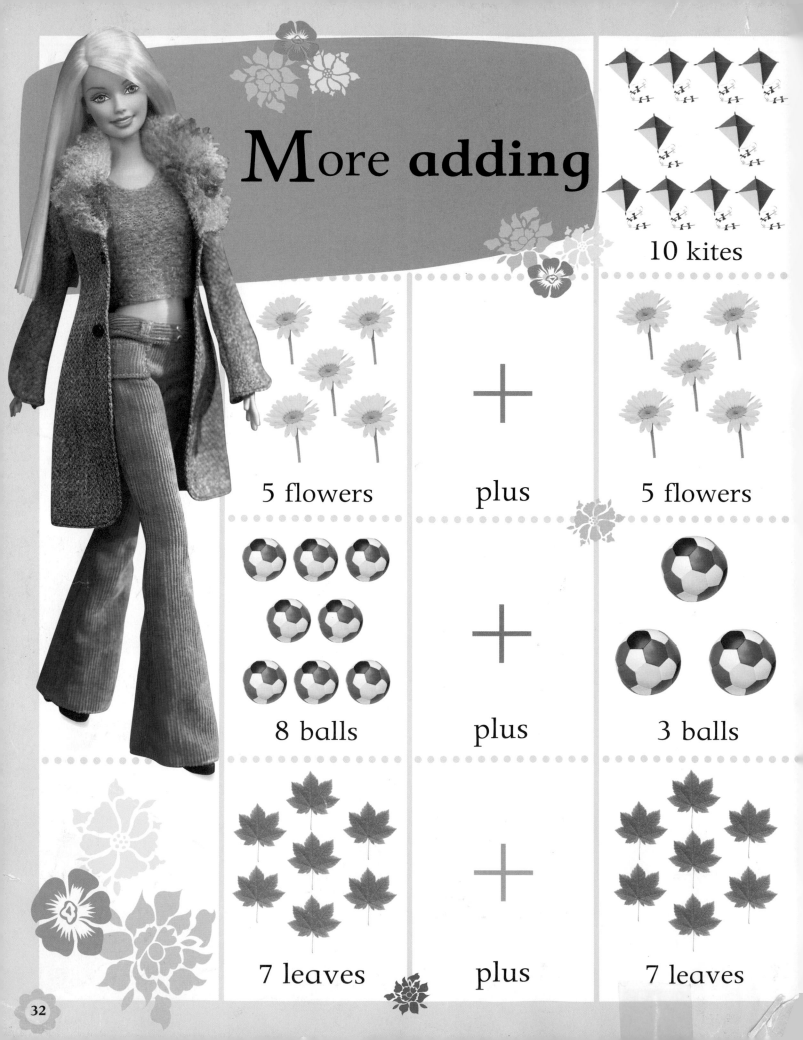

10 kites

5 flowers   plus   5 flowers

8 balls   plus   3 balls

7 leaves   plus   7 leaves

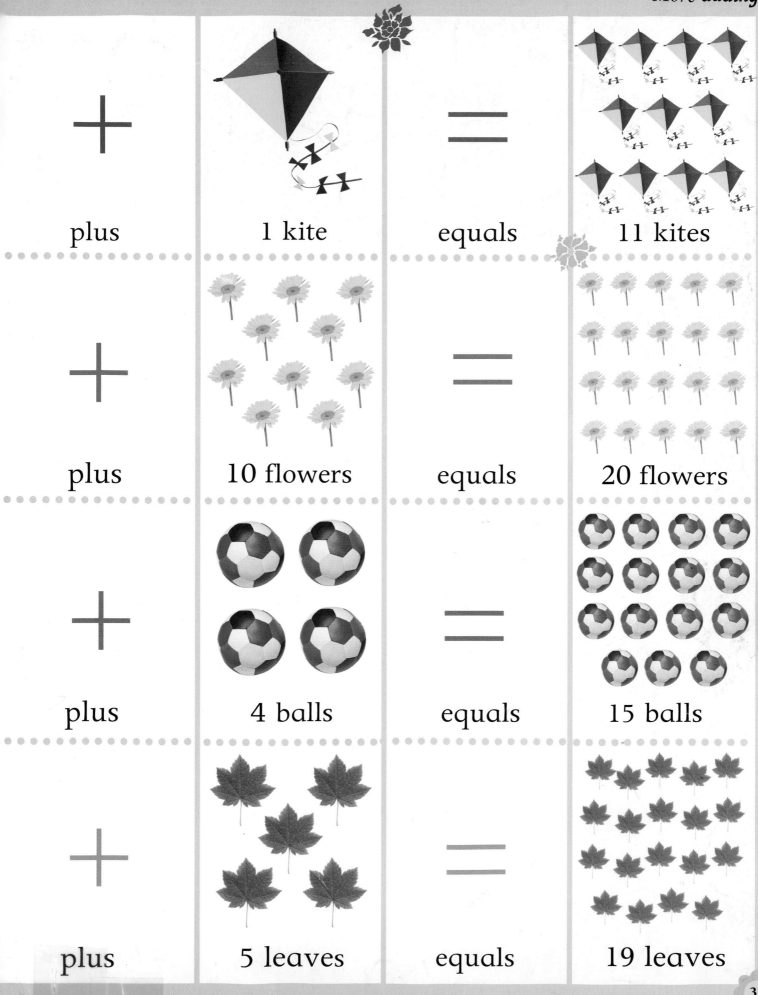

plus	1 kite	equals	11 kites
plus	10 flowers	equals	20 flowers
plus	4 balls	equals	15 balls
plus	5 leaves	equals	19 leaves

Subtracting

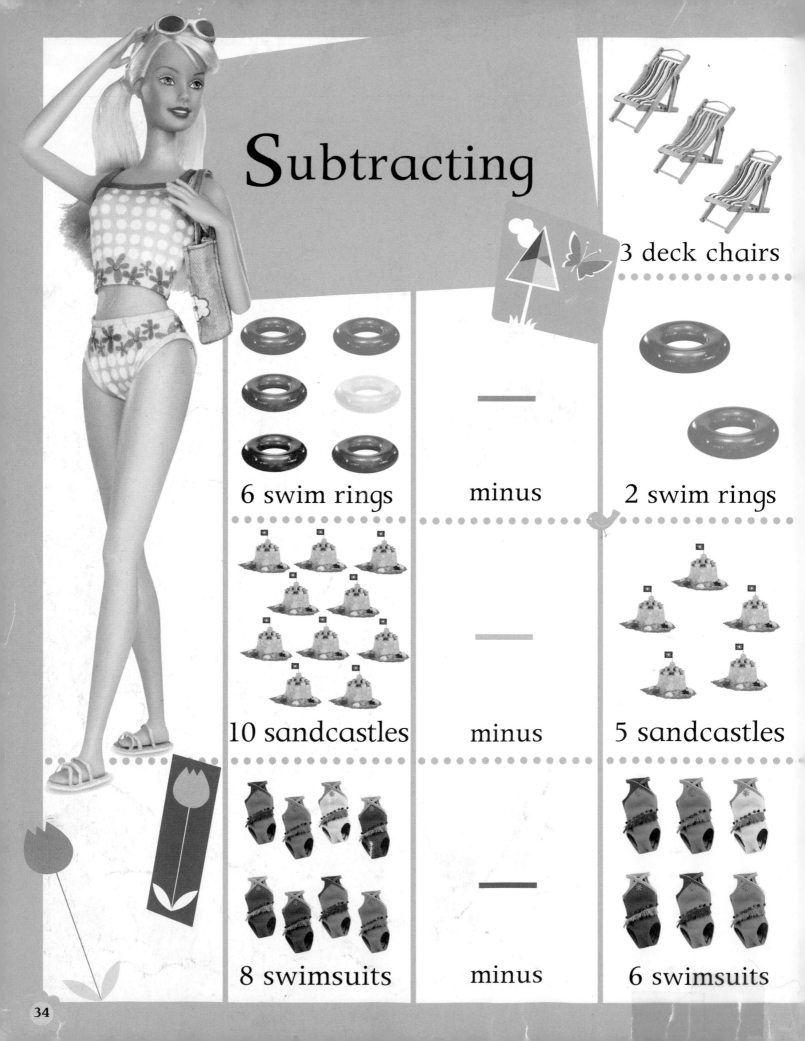

3 deck chairs

6 swim rings   minus   2 swim rings

10 sandcastles   minus   5 sandcastles

8 swimsuits   minus   6 swimsuits

minus

2 deck chairs

equals

1 deck chair

equals

4 swim rings

equals

5 sandcastles

equals

2 swimsuits

Now try these!

Subtraction simply means to take away, or to minus. If there are three deck chairs and you take two deck chairs away, you have one deck chair left.

That means:

$$3 - 2 = 1$$

$$6 - 3 = ?$$

$$8 - 5 = ?$$

$$4 - 3 = ?$$

$$3 - 1 = ?$$

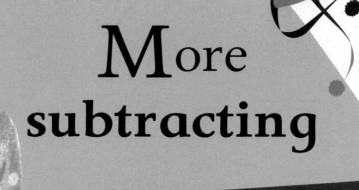

More subtracting

14 scarves

20 umbrellas

12 snowmen

minus

3 snowmen

20 winter hats

minus

6 winter hats

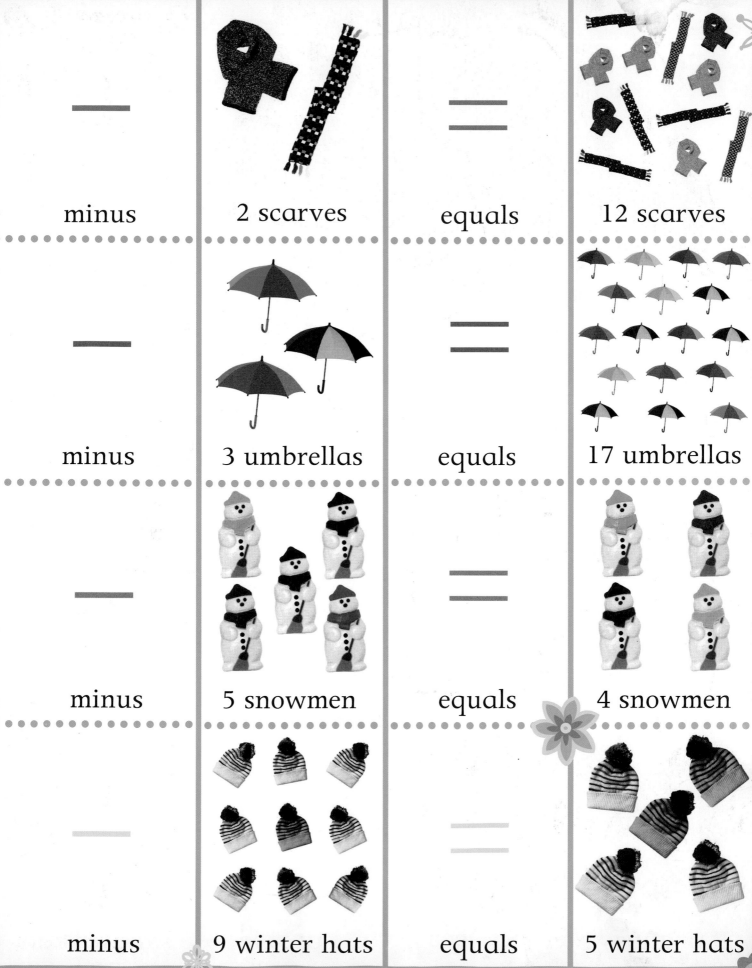

— minus 2 scarves equals 12 scarves

— minus 3 umbrellas equals 17 umbrellas

— minus 5 snowmen equals 4 snowmen

— minus 9 winter hats equals 5 winter hats

Dividing or shared between

4 apples

shared between

6 bananas

shared between

2 people

6 cherries

shared between

3 people

equals

9 oranges

shared between

3 people

equals

6 ribbons

2 apples each

bananas each

h

ch

Simple sharing!

Dividing is another way of saying "shared between." If Barbie has lunch with Teresa and they share six bananas between two people, they would have three bananas each. That means

$$6 \div 2 = 3$$

More dividing

9 tutus

8 leotards

divided by

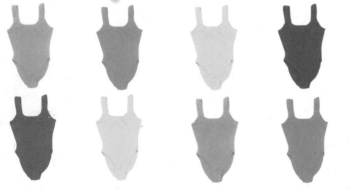

12 barrettes

divided by

÷ **2**  =

divided by

equals 3 ribbons

÷ **3** =

divided by

equals 3 tutus

=

equals 4 leotards

=

equals 4 barrettes

Try it yourself!

Work out the answers to these division problems.

$6 \div 3 = ?$

$8 \div 4 = ?$

$10 \div 2 = ?$

$16 \div 8 = ?$

$10 \div 5 = ?$

$18 \div 2 = ?$

$20 \div 10 = ?$

Counting
by twos

2

8

14

18

4

6

10

12

16

Counting by twos is a great way to start learning your two times table!

20

To find the next number, just add two every time.

Learn the **two** times table!

2
two

2	x	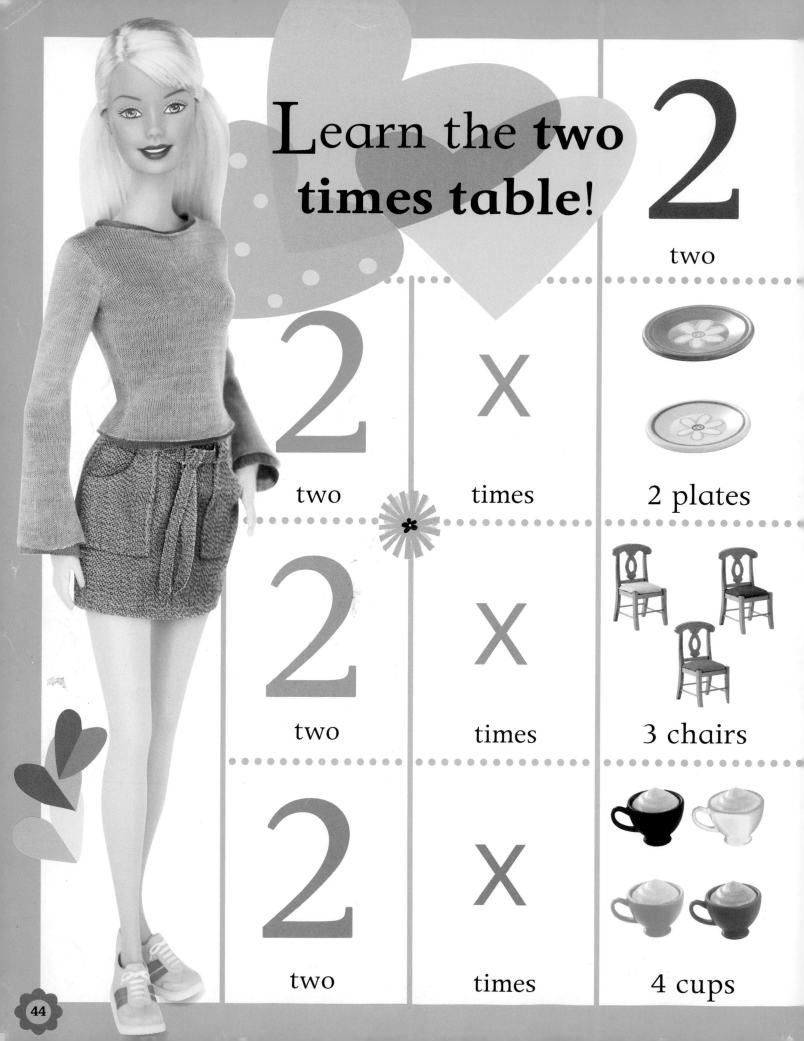
two	times	2 plates
2	x	
two	times	3 chairs
2	x	
two	times	4 cups

44

X

times

1 sofa

= equals

2 sofas

=

equals

4 plates

=

equals

=

equals

Multiplying

Multiplying is a way to add groups with the same number of objects.

2 x 3 means three groups of two objects each.

$$2 + 2 + 2 = 6$$

It doesn't matter which number is first.

$$3 \times 2 = 6$$
$$2 \times 3 = 6$$

Two times table

1 x 2 = 2	7 x 2 = 14
2 x 2 = 4	8 x 2 = 16
3 x 2 = 6	9 x 2 = 18
4 x 2 = 8	10 x 2 = 20
5 x 2 = 10	11 x 2 = 22
6 x 2 = 12	12 x 2 = 24

More multiplying

1 one

2 two

x times

3 three

x times

2 sweatbands

4 four

x times

2 shuttlecocks

= equals

X

times

1 ball

 =

equals

1 ball

1 tennis racket

=

equals

2 tennis rackets

 =

equals

6 sweatbands

8 shuttlecocks

More multiplying!
Can you solve these problems?

$$2 \times 2 = ?$$
$$2 \times 3 = ?$$
$$4 \times 3 = ?$$

Times tables

Times tables are lists of all the ways numbers can be multiplied.

Try learning all the times tables in the back of this book!

Math practice

Good job!
Now you've learned how to count from 1 to 20 and how to add, subtract, multiply, and divide! Here's some more practice problems.

+

add

−

subtract

÷

divide

X

multiply

$5 + 4 = ?$

$15 + 5 = ?$

$12 + 2 = ?$

$10 + 3 = ?$

$16 + 4 = ?$

$19 - 16 = ?$

$12 - 10 = ?$

$17 - 7 = ?$

$10 - 3 = ?$

$16 - 13 = ?$

$20 \div 5 = ?$

$12 \div 2 = ?$

$15 \div 3 = ?$

$20 \div 2 = ?$

$16 \div 4 = ?$

$2 \times 5 = ?$

$3 \times 4 = ?$

$2 \times 8 = ?$

$4 \times 2 = ?$

$5 \times 3 = ?$

1 x table

1	x 1	=	1
2	x 1	=	2
3	x 1	=	3
4	x 1	=	4
5	x 1	=	5
6	x 1	=	6
7	x 1	=	7
8	x 1	=	8
9	x 1	=	9
10	x 1	=	10
11	x 1	=	11
12	x 1	=	12

2 x table

1	x 2	=	2
2	x 2	=	4
3	x 2	=	6
4	x 2	=	8
5	x 2	=	10
6	x 2	=	12
7	x 2	=	14
8	x 2	=	16
9	x 2	=	18
10	x 2	=	20
11	x 2	=	22
12	x 2	=	24

5 x table

1	x 5	=	5
2	x 5	=	10
3	x 5	=	15
4	x 5	=	20
5	x 5	=	25
6	x 5	=	30
7	x 5	=	35
8	x 5	=	40
9	x 5	=	45
10	x 5	=	50
11	x 5	=	55
12	x 5	=	60

6 x table

1	x 6	=	6
2	x 6	=	12
3	x 6	=	18
4	x 6	=	24
5	x 6	=	30
6	x 6	=	36
7	x 6	=	42
8	x 6	=	48
9	x 6	=	54
10	x 6	=	60
11	x 6	=	66
12	x 6	=	72

9 x table

1	x 9	=	9
2	x 9	=	18
3	x 9	=	27
4	x 9	=	36
5	x 9	=	45
6	x 9	=	54
7	x 9	=	63
8	x 9	=	72
9	x 9	=	81
10	x 9	=	90
11	x 9	=	99
12	x 9	=	108

10 x table

1	x 10	=	10
2	x 10	=	20
3	x 10	=	30
4	x 10	=	40
5	x 10	=	50
6	x 10	=	60
7	x 10	=	70
8	x 10	=	80
9	x 10	=	90
10	x 10	=	100
11	x 10	=	110
12	x 10	=	120